Robert Potter

The Relation of Ethics to Religion

An introduction to the Critical Study of Christianity

Robert Potter

The Relation of Ethics to Religion
An introduction to the Critical Study of Christianity

ISBN/EAN: 9783337131227

Printed in Europe, USA, Canada, Australia, Japan

Cover: Foto ©Lupo / pixelio.de

More available books at **www.hansebooks.com**

THE RELATION

OF

ETHICS TO RELIGION

An Introduction to the Critical Study of Christianity

BY

ROBERT POTTER, M.A.

LECTURER ON CHRISTIAN EVIDENCES IN TRINITY COLLEGE, MELBOURNE;
EXAMINER IN LOGIC AND PHILOSOPHY IN THE UNIVERSITY OF
MELBOURNE; CANON OF S. PAUL'S, MELBOURNE.

LONDON
MACMILLAN AND CO
GEORGE ROBERTSON AND COMPANY
MELBOURNE AND SYDNEY
1888

To

H. H. P. HANDFIELD,

Canon of S. Paul's, Melbourne,

This Book is Dedicated.

I have equipped my little barque
To try the seas, and now
I wish, before she sails, to mark
A name upon her prow;

A name that, if some kindly fate
Befriend her sail and oar,
May lend an honour to the freight
She carries to the shore;

A name of one that, if the ship
Should never make the land,
Will comfort with a brother's grip
The stranded sailor's hand.

I well believe, my dear old friend,
For either need of mine,
No name, that I could choose, would lend
So sure a pledge as thine.

R. P.

"THE THINGS THAT WE IMMEDIATELY KNOW ABOUT ARE MERE PHENOMENA, NOT FOR US ONLY, BUT IN THEIR OWN NATURE AND WITHOUT OUR INTERFERENCE; AND THESE THINGS, FINITE AS THEY ARE, ARE APPROPRIATELY DESCRIBED WHEN WE SAY THAT THEIR BEING IS ESTABLISHED NOT ON THEMSELVES BUT ON THE DIVINE AND UNIVERSAL IDEA."

TABLE OF CONTENTS.

	PAGE
PREFACE	11

INTRODUCTION.

A rule of conduct is of the essence of Christianity:	1, 2
Its kindred and ancestry are indicated by such rule:	2, 3
Hebrew prophecy and Greek philosophy:	3
Natural and revealed religion: the distinction between them exists in virtue of the presence or absence of a characteristic mark.	4, 5
The essence of religion, revealed or natural, is the moral idea.	5
The sense of wonder and the instinct of worship must be exercised in subordination to the moral idea. The question, therefore, "What is righteousness?" lies at the threshold of all inquiries about religion.	6

CHAPTER I.

THE SEARCH FOR A CRITERION OF RIGHTEOUSNESS.

1. Every rule of conduct implies the many and the one. - 7
2. The definition of righteousness must have reference to both. - 8
3. The development of our capacities in due order and harmony: need of a criterion to determine what is "due." - 8–10

Table of Contents.

PAGE

4. Can we construct such a criterion out of happiness? Not unless we define righteousness as that conduct which proceeds always in the line of least resistance. Otherwise, we must assume that the world is made on a preconceived system, and that such system is favourable to righteousness. Nor even then can we construct such a criterion out of happiness, if we admit that the way of duty is ever "not joyous but grievous." Result of the attempt to construct out of happiness a criterion of righteousness. 10, 11

5. Result not fruitless, for it emphasizes for us the antecedent universal which is implied in the contrasted existence of the many and the one. - - 11, 12

6. Can we find the requisite criterion in conscience? Not in the individual conscience, for that is subject to illusions and changes. Origin of such illusions, and remedies. - - - - - 12-14

7. The conscience of humanity is also subject to changes, but the study of these discloses a significant fact: the balance of these changes is in one direction. 15, 16

8. The trend which is thus indicated exhibits a command which the conscience of humanity recognizes and acknowledges itself bound to obey. This result shows us in what direction we are to look for the criterion that we need, but it indicates a principle which transcends humanity. - - - - 16

9. Relation of pleasure and pain to morality. Mr. Herbert Spencer and J. S. Mill in contrast. - 17-19

10. Results of disobedience to the command which the conscience of humanity recognizes and acknowledges itself bound to obey. - - - - 20

11. Approximate criterion of righteousness derivable from the preceding considerations: - - 21, 22

12. This criterion may be improved by the study on a large scale of the relation of pleasure and pain to an assumed morality. The twofold assumption which this improved criterion implies. - - 22, 23
13. Contrast between revealed and natural religion, in respect of the criterion of right conduct. - 23, 24

CHAPTER II.
THE BASIS OF THE UNITY OF ALL THINGS.

14. We presume that all things form a coherent system. - 25
15. Such a presumption is not capable of inductive proof. 26, 27
16. J. S. Mill and Mr. Bain on the "uniformity of nature" and its relation to experience. - - - 28
17. The presumption in question can only be established by proving that without it thought is impossible. - 29
18. Further development of its meaning. - - - 30
19. It implies the presence of an idea co-extensive with the whole system of things. - - - - 31
20. The statement of monotheism and the statement of the law of universal causation involve identical propositions; monotheism, therefore, cannot be established by inductive reasoning. - - - - 32
21. The argument from design, although of great value, is of no avail to establish absolute monotheism 32, 33
22. But monotheism may, nevertheless, be established as a necessary postulate of speculative thought, for every state of consciousness implies a standard, in virtue of its correspondence with which, it is valid. 33, 34
23. Objection and answer. - - - - - 34
24. Further objection and answer. - - - 35, 36
25. Recapitulation. - - - - - - 36

26. The thing-in-itself, apart from consciousness, cannot be that standard ; for the thing-in-itself, apart from consciousness, if potentially something, is actually nothing : - - - - - - 37
27. The thing-in-itself is a state of consciousness, not of yours nor of mine, but of a consciousness which is universal. Either there is a universal consciousness, to which every particular consciousness is related and subordinate, or else all our perceptions and thoughts are without any real solidity or coherence. - - - - - - 37
28. Kant and "dogmatic idealism." - - 38, 39
29. T. R. Green and Kant in contrast - - - 39
30. Tendency in some quarters to separate ethics from religion. Consequences to both. - - - 40
31. The imperative of conscience, and the power which is behind nature. - - - - - 41
32. The alternative of absolute monotheism. - 41, 42
33. Certain illogical compromises, theological and philosophical. Relation of monism to monotheism. 42, 43

CHAPTER III.

THE WORLD AND THE SELF-LIMITED SUPREME.

34. The relation of the argument from design to the conclusion of the preceding argument : - - - 44
35. The conclusion of the argument from design is already implicit in the primary postulate of thought. The argument possesses, however, an independent value : 44, 45
36. Evolution and design. - - - - 45, 46
37. Application of argument from design to the establishment of a scientific doctrine ; - - - 46
38. Application of the same argument to the establishment of a doctrine of religion. The criticism of this application by J. S. Mill. This criticism criticised. 47-49

Table of Contents. ix

PAGE

39. The conclusion from the argument from design.   49, 50
40. How affected by the doctrine of evolution. -   50, 51
41. Time and design. - - - -   51, 52
42. Is the Supreme Being to be identified with the maker of the world? The problem does not emerge in the Old Testament. But it appears in the Oriental religions and in the gnostic and allied heresies;   52, 53
43. Also in modern philosophy, Spencer and Mill.   53, 54
44. Statement of the problem. Is it self-contradictory to say that, although the Supreme Cause is by His very nature above all conditions, yet we see Him, as the Maker, working under conditions? -   54–56
45. No, if the conditions are self-imposed; but in that case we have to find an answer to the question, "Why does the Infinite Being submit Himself to conditions?" - - - - -   56, 57
46. Considerations which indicate where the answer is to be looked for. - - - -   57, 58
47. All phenomena do not of necessity imply the self-limitation of the Absolute, but the existence of subordinate self-conscious intelligences does imply such limitation. - - - -   58, 59
48. If the subordinate self-conscious intelligence is not self-determining, its existence is no adequate cause for the self-limitation of the Supreme. -   59, 60
49. "Virtue" and "freedom," and "the origin of evil."   60, 61
50. First stage of the self-limitation of the Supreme: 61, 62
51. Second stage of the self-limitation of the Supreme: -   62
52. Third stage; the manifestation of "the sons of God" is the final cause of the self-limitation of the Supreme.   62, 63
*53. This conclusion, however, assumes that the absolute power which controls the universe is in harmony with the conscience of humanity. This assumption remains to be considered - - -   63, 64

* The number of this section has been accidentally omitted from the text.

CHAPTER IV.

FREEDOM AND EVIL.

PAGE

54 and 55. Recapitulation and summary of results. The final question proposed. - - - 65–67

56. Preliminary consideration, Is moral freedom illusion? Determinism: - - - - 68–70

57. Difficulties in the way of accepting the determinist conclusion: - - - - - 70–72

58. The determinist argument yields an alternative conclusion, viz.: *If the free-will of man cannot be part of the controlled system, it must be part of the controlling idea.* - - - - - 72, 73

59. Kant, Spencer, and Green. - - - 73–75

60. Other processes of reasoning issue in the same result. 75, 76

61. Relations of "matter" and "organism" to the free agency of the creature. - - - 76–78

62. The alternative to the conclusion that God is good. 78, 79

63. Evidence of "nature." - - - - 79–81

64. Evidence of "the moral paradox." - - 81, 82

65. Argument on the other side: Omnipotence and evil. Answer. - - - - - 82, 83

66. Is it worth while? - - - - - 83

67. The "future life" and the "goodness of God." 83, 84

68. Infliction of pain. Sympathy. To create was to be crucified. - - - - - - 84

69. The last words of "natural religion," and the demand which it makes of revelation. - - 84, 85

PREFACE.

THE endeavour to find a criterion of good, forces upon us the search for God; for, whether we define goodness in terms of happiness, or happiness in terms of goodness, either definition implies a principle which transcends experience. And the search for that principle proves to be a search for God. When we have found in God such a principle, we are constrained to inquire how there comes to be anything but goodness in the universe. And in the analysis of goodness as a quality of the creature we see the way to an answer; for goodness implies the power of choice, and the power of choice implies freedom, and freedom implies the possibility of evil.

When we have before us God and the freedom of the creature, we begin to see that the existence of the world as it is, implies the self-limitation of the Supreme; and we are constrained to inquire, Why should the Supreme so limit Himself? As soon as we find an answer to that question we are in a position to enter upon a critical study of revealed religion.

To work out the steps by which we arrive at this position is the purpose of the following pages.

THE RELATION OF ETHICS TO RELIGION.

INTRODUCTION.

CHRISTIANITY in the days of its earliest history was known as "The Way."* Such a name implies that the religion of Christ was understood to prescribe a rule of life or conduct for its followers. And it is essential to the purpose of this treatise to make sure, as far as possible, of that rule and its meaning. And there is

ERRATUM.

Page 82, section 65—*For* "in order to increase happiness," *read* "in order to increase goodness."

would indicate both. The great Hebrew prophets of

* Acts xix. 23. † S. Matthew v. 20.
‡ 1 S. John iii. 10.

THE RELATION OF ETHICS TO RELIGION.

INTRODUCTION.

CHRISTIANITY in the days of its earliest history was known as " The Way."* Such a name implies that the religion of Christ was understood to prescribe a rule of life or conduct for its followers. And it is essential to the purpose of this treatise to make sure, as far as possible, of that rule and its meaning. There is no doubt about the terms in which it must be stated, whatever difference of opinion there may be about the meaning of those terms. For the rule is " righteousness." The unrighteous man cannot belong to the kingdom of God.† " Whosoever doeth not righteousness is not of God."‡

And in respect of this rule Christianity makes no abrupt beginning. On the contrary, if we had no other means of ascertaining its kindred and ancestry, this would indicate both. The great Hebrew prophets of

* Acts xix. 23. † S. Matthew v. 20.
‡ 1 S. John iii. 10.

the eighth century before Christ were pre-eminently preachers of righteousness. "What doth Jehovah require of thee," says one of them, " but to do justly, and to love mercy, and to walk humbly with thy God?"* And the greatest of the Greek philosophers were also pre-eminently preachers of righteousness. Plato teaches that "justice is the virtue of the soul," whereby the soul lives well, and "he who lives well is blessed and happy."† "And justice is better than injustice, insomuch that whether gods or men see it or not, the one is in itself a blessing and the other a bane."‡

When we are thus put in mind of the kindred and ancestry of Christianity, when we think of its relationship alike to Hebrew prophecy and to Greek philosophy, we have before us the distinction between natural and revealed religion. And it will be well to turn our attention to this distinction before we begin the attempt to define that which is common to the things distinguished.

It is a distinction of long standing. It was known to S. Paul.§ It was familiar to the early Christian apologists. It has long been a commonplace of the Christian teacher. Bishop Butler assumes it both in the title and in the construction of his great work. It is a real distinction, but, like many other real distinctions, it does not exist in virtue of any well-defined line which can be drawn between the things distinguished.

---

* Micah vi. 8.   † "Republic," i. (Davies and Vaughan).
‡ "Republic," ii. (Davies and Vaughan).   § Romans ii. 14.

It exists in virtue of certain contrasted characteristics. A painter will shade red and blue together so that you cannot draw a line and say, here the red ends and here the blue begins. And yet you will always be able to take two points and say, it is surely red here and surely blue there. Suppose we admit the presence of a human element in Hebrew prophecy, and of a divine element in Greek philosophy, and suppose we go on to affirm that there is more of the divine than of the human in the former, and more of the human than of the divine in the latter, we do not therefore arrive at any hard and fast line of distinction; for we cannot exactly say in either case where the human ends and where the divine begins. And if we look about us at the present time, and survey the great variety of opinion that prevails, we find ourselves less able than ever to draw any such line. Moralists who would quite earnestly repudiate for themselves the character of the Christian teacher are nevertheless powerfully influenced by Christian teaching; they will themselves not venture to affirm that their doctrine would be what it is had it not been for Christianity. And most Christians, on the other hand, would gladly admit the truth of the saying attributed to Tertullian, " O human soul, who art *by nature* a Christian." Bishop Butler himself (although, as I have said, the distinction between natural and revealed religion is assumed in the "Analogy,") nevertheless admits quite freely that no hard and fast line can be drawn. His words are these: " Persons' notions of what is natural will be enlarged in proportion to their greater knowledge of the works of God and the dispensations of His providence; nor is there any absurdity in supposing that there may be beings in the universe whose capacities and knowledge and views may be so extensive as that the whole Christian dispensation may to them appear *natural, i.e.*, analogous or conformable to God's dealing with other parts of His creation."* The religion which we call natural is itself revealed, for nature is a revelation of God, and revealed religion is itself natural in the sense that it is throughout in accordance with the laws of the universe.

Nevertheless there is as vivid a distinction between natural and revealed religion as there is between blue and red. We learn always from God. But sometimes we are conscious of the fact that we are learning from Him, and sometimes we seem to ourselves to be simply investigating the facts. The characteristic of what we call revealed religion is the consciousness of being taught of God. Religion from which such consciousness is absent is natural religion. The disciple of natural religion thinks about God. The disciple of revealed religion communes with God.

This distinction makes a very great difference when we come to inquire whether any religion be true or untrue. The religion which assumes to be natural, if untrue, may be only a mistake, and if the

---

* "Analogy," i. (1).

The Relation of Ethics to Religion. 5

investigation on which it is founded be continued, the mistake may be corrected, and the religion may become more and more nearly true. The religion which assumes to be revealed, if untrue, must be founded on either illusion or imposture, and the continuance of either can only make bad worse.

Religion, then, whether it be revealed or natural, provides a rule of conduct for men, and that rule is righteousness. The essence of religion is the moral idea. The sense of wonder and the instinct of worship are indeed included in religion, but only as dependent on the moral idea. Wonder and worship divorced from the moral idea degrade humanity. It is true that a system of government which is utterly devoid of righteousness, and which is built upon mere self-regard, may nevertheless, if it act with power, precision, and effect, draw to itself the wonder and even the worship of men. So may a school of art whose essential thought is beastly, if only it possess a special excellence of style or design in speech or colour. The whole world may wonder after the beast, but the world which wonders after the beast is a degraded world, all the more degraded for its very capacity of wonder.

But the moral idea distinguishes and exalts humanity, and in doing so it introduces men to the worthiest objects both of wonder and, of worship ; of wonder, for the soul which, independent of external constraint, or in defiance of it, is a law unto itself, is the most wonderful thing of which we have experience;* of worship, for although beauty is admirable and power is terrible, goodness only is adorable.

It is clear, therefore, that the question, "What is righteousness?" lies at the threshold of all inquiries about religion. All such inquiries are a mere groping in the dark unless we know what righteousness is. And as it is the purpose of this book to serve as an introduction to the study of revealed religion, the question "What is righteousness?" must be answered in the first place, and the question "What is righteousness?" implies, of course, the question "What is unrighteousness?" We must make up our minds therefore on these questions of "good" and "evil;" questions which are at least coeval with humanity and co-extensive with it; not only before we can inquire with any prospect of success what is religion, and what are the evidences of religion, but before we can understand what such inquiries mean.

And in putting this question we must try to take nothing for granted, except such postulates as may be given in the very fact that the question is being put; and we must not assume any postulate as being so given without careful examination.

---

* Kant (Abbott's translation)—"Metaphysic of Morals" (70); "Methodology of Pure Practical Reason" (313), conclusion.

CHAPTER I.

(1.) ANY rule of conduct, whatsoever it be, implies the many and the one. For conduct is, in fact, the action of each with reference to the others : unrelated existence, when you try to think it, proves to have no meaning. The individual self is indeed the unit of the community ; but it is neither more nor less true that the individual exists in virtue of his relation to the community than that the community exists on the basis of the individual. If it be asked which of them comes first, I think the answer must be that neither can have existed before the other. There is a discussion in philology whether the word or the sentence came first, and I think that the answer that is coming to be accepted is something like this ; that the antecedent of the word and the sentence was neither and yet was both. Perhaps the natural history of being and of becoming may at last yield a parallel answer. The antecedent alike of the individual and of the community must somehow have included both, and the process of differentiation is beyond our ken. At least we have no concern with it here. Our point at present is that you cannot isolate either thought ; you cannot lay down a rule of conduct for the individual without taking into account his relation to the community ; and you cannot lay down a rule for the community without taking into account the individual.

(2.) Conduct implies what is called self-determination. If we are speaking of the way in which a man is forced against his will to go, we do not call that his "conduct." We mean by his conduct the way in which he chooses to go. But every man has in him undeveloped capacities, and right conduct is the choice in action to fulfil those capacities in due order and harmony. An acorn, it is true, has undeveloped capacities as well as a man, and it is right in the case of the acorn, as well as in the case of the man, that such capacities should be fulfilled. But the acorn has no power of choice, and so we do not attribute right conduct to it. The man has the power of choice, and so we do attribute right conduct to him. But we cannot define right conduct as the endeavour on the part of each simply to fulfil in due order and harmony all the capacities of his nature. For conduct, as we have seen, implies the many and the one: and to define conduct so would be as far as possible to ignore the many. We must define right conduct to be such conduct as tends to the fulfilment in due order and harmony of the capacities of the nature of each, in such manner as to give the most possible help to the others in the like fulfilment of the capacities of their nature.

(3.) Here, however, a difficulty presents itself. What is *due order and harmony?* The words imply that each capacity has its own place and its own value, different place and different value. Some are higher and some are lower. Some capacities have a natural tendency to pass away. This becomes apparent either by their gradual decline through a long series of ages, or by the fact that if they are cultivated beyond a certain point they destroy the race that exerts them. The phenomena of natural history prove also that capacities have passed away wholly, and that the race which has lost them has nevertheless risen in the scale of being.

But it is one thing to prove that each of our capacities has a place and value of its own, and quite another thing to prove which of them is of the most value, and which of them should have the first place. It may be, for all that we can say beforehand, that the capacity which passes is the better and that which endures the worse. It may be better, and not worse, that this or that race should perish,

> "All our life is mixed with death,
> And who knoweth which is best?"

But there is a difference, and the fact that there is gives meaning to the words, "*due order and harmony.*" The fulfilment of our capacities in due order and harmony must be taken to imply three things— (I.) precedence to be given to some of them above others; (II.) caution that such precedence of some does not imply the abrupt destruction of the others; (III.) recognition, nevertheless, of the evanescent nature of some capacities; not evanescent, it may be, with reference to the history of the individual or to one stage of being, but with reference to the history of being throughout all stages.* It follows, then, that we stand in need of a criterion whereby we may decide what capacities are to take precedence. Given such criterion, and then the caution (II.) and the recognition (III.) follow as matter of course.

(4.) Is there any such criterion given in human nature? Can we find such a criterion in happiness? Shall we say that the conduct which upon the whole results in the most happiness for each is the right conduct for each? Or shall we say that the conduct which upon the whole results in the most happiness for the community is the right conduct for each individual? No criterion such as we need can be so constructed. For anything that we can say at the present stage of this inquiry, either or both of the above statements may be true. It may be that "virtue" and "fortune" are actually at one, that righteousness and happiness will ultimately prove to be coincident. But to assume this is to assume that the world is made on a preconceived system; that the universe is, in fact, one; and it is also to assume that the system on which the world is made is favourable to righteousness. We shall have presently to examine these assumptions, and to see what reason there is for making them. But we have no right to make them just yet. And even suppose we do make

* See S. Matt. xxii. 30.

them, still we cannot construct a criterion of right conduct out of happiness. For, unless we declare unhesitatingly that right conduct is neither more nor less than the conduct which proceeds in the line of least resistance, we shall have to admit that the way of righteousness is often " not joyous, but grievous." Whatsoever we suppose the plan of the world to be, and whether we regard righteousness as an end in itself, or merely as a means to happiness, we shall have to admit that it is only on the whole, and not in detail, that righteousness and happiness coincide. And the details in which they are not coincident are so many that a rule of conduct constructed out of such coincidence can be of no avail at all for our guidance. The effort to construct out of happiness a criterion of righteousness results in the conclusion that either there is no such thing as righteousness, or else that, if there be, righteousness in many of the details of life is not coincident with happiness.

(5.) Yet the effort is not quite futile, for it lays emphasis on the fact that there is something which each of us tends to seek, which he calls his happiness; and my neighbour's happiness, considered by itself, is never absolutely coincident with my happiness, and my neighbour and I are members of a community, and the happiness of the community is never absolutely identical with what I call my happiness, or with what any of my neighbours calls his, or with the sum of it all together. But, as we have seen, the individual and the community imply an antecedent which somehow includes both, and the tendency of that antecedent stands no doubt in relation to the tendencies of each individual and of the whole community. And in it we might fairly expect to find their differences adjusted. The varying ends of each and all, in which each and all seek their happiness, must find their only coincident fulfilment in the end of that which precedes and includes each and all. And if we knew what that end is, it might be worth while to inquire whether we might not find in it the criterion of righteousness of which we are in search. Meanwhile it remains clear that unless, as I have said, we define righteousness as that conduct which proceeds in the line of least resistance, we cannot construct out of happiness a criterion of righteousness without the assumption of some principle which transcends mere human nature. For if happiness be a test of righteousness, and if right conduct does not always proceed in the line of least resistance, then we must either assume that the world is constructed upon a system, and that a system which "makes for righteousness," or else we must refer ourselves to the antecedent universal which is implied in the contrasted existence of the many and the one.

(6.) But if we cannot find in happiness a criterion of righteousness, can we find such a criterion in conscience? Not, certainly, in the individual conscience. For this individual conscience differs from that, and comes in time to differ from itself. And yet these very differences provide us with a new point of departure in our search for a criterion of righteousness. Here is a fact which, however it became so, is as much a part of our human nature as our sight is. The imperative of conscience cannot be ignored. Why should we ever distrust it? For the same reason that makes us distrustful sometimes of our sight: because by a comparison of results we discover that it is liable to illusion. It cannot be made a test until itself be tested, and a very brief inquiry into the nature of the illusions to which it is liable proves that the individual conscience cannot be so tested as to become itself an absolutely trustworthy test. For the imperative of conscience is unconditional. But it is our nature to calculate beforehand the consequences of our actions, and we are constantly tempted to allow such calculations to affect the judgement of conscience. As Kant would say, we often put the hypothetical imperative in the place of the categorical. And the frequent intervention of these hypothetical imperatives tends to darken conscience. And suppose we endeavour to dismiss all considerations of consequence, and to act in disregard of them, we cannot by such effort deliver the individual conscience from illusion. For, in the first place, we never can be sure that we have really dismissed them, and we are often led blindly by some forecast of consequences just when we think that we have defied consequence. And, in the second place, while conscience remains unenlightened we may be doing wrong, "in scorn of consequence," instead of right. And it may be that the very consequences that we scorn are the means provided for its enlightenment. For if the universe be one there will be a correspondence upon the whole between the action and its consequences. And such correspondence, on the whole, if we could but get a view of it, could not but help to enlighten conscience, although many consequences in detail would still have to be disregarded. But when we endeavour to distinguish between consequences on the whole and consequences in detail, when we say of any result in particular, "You cannot judge from this; it will be found to be neutralized by the result in general," we are undertaking, it may be, a very difficult analysis, and one in which we may blunder fatally. And, in the third place, when we are most firmly determined not to be swayed by the fear of consequences, we often overshoot the mark, and are swayed by the fear of being swayed by them. It seems, then, that the endeavour to "follow right in scorn of consequence" is usually difficult, and sometimes morally dangerous, although to abstain from making it is always morally fatal.

(7.) It seems, then, that we cannot find in the individual conscience an absolutely trustworthy test of right conduct. But is there not a conscience of the community distinct from the conscience of the individual, just as there is a happiness of the community which is distinct from the happiness of the individual? Undoubtedly there is, and as it is in the case of happiness so it is in the case of conscience. The conscience of the community is not a compromise between the conscience of this individual and of that, and of the other, nor is it the sum of them; the conscience of the community and the conscience of the individual stand related to each other in virtue of the common antecedent of the many and the one.

Can we find in the conscience of the community an absolutely trustworthy test of right conduct? No, for the conscience of the community is also liable to illusions and changes. But when we come to examine those changes a very suggestive result emerges. The changes in the individual conscience are now in this direction and now in that, and the individual passes from the stage of history so soon that there is no time to see if there be any decisive balance on this side or that. The changes in the conscience of the community are also now in this direction and now in that, but the community continues; there is time for such a balance to become apparent. If we stand for a minute by the seaside the waves appear only to be going and returning, there is no progress either way. If we watch them for twenty minutes we see that the tide is coming in. We cannot say how high it will rise, but we know that it is rising. And so if we compare an earlier age with a later, and that with a later still, we discover a very decisive trend in the progress of the human conscience. For instance, conscience at a very early period recognizes a duty of every member of the tribe to every other member of the tribe, but none beyond. Later on conscience recognizes a duty of Greek to Greek, but none of Greek to barbarian. Later on still conscience recognizes the duty of every man to every man. The laws of war, the administration of justice, national and international, the institution of slavery, provide a variety of illustrations. Changes in public morality are being made from time to time, and made in all directions, but only those continue which are made in one direction. The changed ideal is first the aspiration of a single individual, then a counsel of perfection for the few, at last a commonplace of public opinion.

(8.) This gradual progress in one direction is an ascertained fact, and it is a fact of the utmost importance to our present inquiry. I do not say that it provides us with a decisive criterion of right conduct, but it shows us where such a criterion is to be found. The absolute high-water mark is not in view, but we know now in what direction to look for it. The command,

"Move upward, working out the beast,"

has been spoken, and mankind has recognized it, and knows that it must be obeyed.

But the question was, Is there a criterion of right conduct given in human nature? And the result so far is altogether in the negative. The trend which we have discovered in humanity is towards a goal which is beyond humanity. We cannot construct out of conscience, any more than out of the desire of happiness, a criterion of right conduct, without the assumption of some principle which transcends mere human nature.

(9.) The result at which we have arrived entitles us to affirm that righteousness cannot be defined in terms of pleasure. We might, indeed, enter at this point on a fruitless and wearisome discussion. It might be said that the righteous man, even if he be in pain, derives more pleasure from his righteousness than the unrighteous man, even if he be not in pain, derives from his unrighteousness. And the meaning which would be probably intended is true; but the language is misleading. For it is the same as to say that pleasure is the opposite, not of pain, but of unrighteousness, and that is to play fast and loose with words. If self-pleasing be the end sought, it may always be much more easily attained by the surrender of such aspirations as demand a more difficult satisfaction, and the substitution for them of aspirations which are more easily satisfied. I admit that pleasure and pain stand in relation to morality, and that such relation arises out of their effect on the preservation and destruction of life. And the argument founded upon this relation and effect will become of some importance to us by-and-by. But we cannot safely take it into account, or the general truths on which it is based, if we define righteousness in terms of pleasure. Mr. Herbert Spencer tells us that "the non-recognition of these general truths vitiates moral speculation at large."* But if we understand the phrase "at large"

* "Data of Ethics," section 37.

as I think the context requires, we cannot admit it. If right and wrong are inherently independent of pleasure and pain, no mistaken theory of the relation of pleasure and pain to right and wrong can vitiate moral speculation at large. If, indeed, we discover in the order of nature indications of a tendency to associate, under any circumstances, pleasure with righteousness, and pain with wrong-doing, the disregard of such indications will no doubt vitiate moral speculation in detail. But as long as a direct conflict of pleasure with righteousness is not only possible, but actual, so long pleasure cannot be a guide to righteousness, and the effect of pleasure and pain on the preservation and destruction of life is an effect which the righteous man must be prepared to disregard. Mr. Herbert Spencer, in the context from which I have just quoted, speaks of those who accept pleasure and submit to pain, and he says :—" Leaving out of view the indirect results, the direct results are that one has moved a step away from death and the other has moved a step towards death." Even if we admit all this, it still remains to be said (I.) that the indirect results are so many and so complicated that they will not endure to be left out of sight in practice ; and (II.) even supposing that pleasure always leads to life, and that pain always leads to death, yet life is not in every imaginable event preferable to death. If Ahriman and not Ormuzd should prevail, then death would be better than life. In such a case, and of such a one, J. S. Mill would say, " If I must go to hell for not worshipping him, then to hell I will go." Pleasure is better than pain and life is better than death only if pleasure and life be consistent with righteousness. I say, then, that the result at which we have arrived entitles us to affirm that righteousness cannot be defined in terms of pleasure. We have discovered somewhat in the common conscience of mankind which appears outwardly as progress in a definite direction. The relationship between man and brute is a fact which it did not need the doctrine of evolution to establish. But the progress which we have discovered in the conscience of humanity is away from the brute. And such progress cannot be made without much renunciation of pleasure. The command,

"Move upward, working out the beast,"

is a command of which the fulfilment involves effort and pain. And for some of us at least it would retain its urgency even if it involved for such effort and pain no prospect of compensation. It may, indeed, involve the fullest compensation; it may involve the highest degree of happiness in the ultimate issue. No doubt it will if the universe be one, and if the principle of its unity be in favour of righteousness. But if we are not to obey the command until we have acquired such knowledge as shall enable us to transform this "may" into "must," then we cannot but set it aside, and adopt instead of it a rule of conduct which may be trusted to result in some sort of satisfaction, which, though perhaps not very durable, will at least have a recognized and ascertainable value.

(10.) Nevertheless, the command in question, from whatsoever source it comes, or how difficult soever it may be to obey it, has been spoken : it is in some sort recognized in all philosophies, and was recognized, no doubt, before there was any philosophy at all. It is perhaps more fully recognized now than ever, for it is the doctrine of evolution in the imperative mood. It is a command, moreover, which has been obeyed, and the effects of obeying which are manifest. But it is also a command which has been disobeyed. And it has been disobeyed for periods long antecedent, no doubt, to the earliest epochs of which we have any sort of knowledge. And to disobey it must produce effects. He who, in defiance of the command, prefers the lower but easier and more assured satisfaction, sets out upon a course of development of which we can see the direction, but not the end. We must be prepared to admit that there may be creatures in the universe who find their highest satisfaction in transgressing it : their highest satisfaction, that is to say, in sacrificing their own less brutal to their more brutal capacities, and in thwarting the fulfilment of the less brutal capacities of other creatures. We must admit, indeed, that the order of the universe, if it be one, and if it is to preserve its unity, implies a power to work such creatures out of existence, or else to alter their disposition towards themselves and their fellow-creatures, although we cannot say how such power is to operate, or how long its operation is to take. And we have yet to inquire, Is the order of the universe one, and is the principle of its unity in harmony with the command which we are considering?

(11.) But before we attempt any such inquiry it will be well to recapitulate a little. How near are we, let us ask, to a trustworthy criterion of right conduct, a criterion that will enable us to decide which of our various capacities ought at any time to receive the first place in the order in which we seek to fulfil them?

(I.) Our attention has been directed to the fact that the conscience of humanity has been making progress from age to age in a definite direction, and that such progress is made in obedience to a command which the conscience of humanity recognizes. And such command, howsoever given, points to a goal beyond humanity, and implies a principle which transcends mere human nature. (II.) We have also observed that the conscience of the individual is habitually blinded by the calculation of consequences, and that such calculations of consequences must be set aside if the indications of the individual conscience are to be taken as a test of right conduct. We have learned, nevertheless, that such disregard of consequences involves a task which is critical and dangerous.

It seems now that we may combine these results. The calculation of consequences, which blinds conscience, is made upon the basis of pleasure and pain. Will the results of such actions, one asks, increase or diminish the happiness of oneself, one's friends, and one's fellow-creatures? Suppose we make our calculation on a different basis. Suppose we ask, Will the results of such action be in harmony with the progress which the conscience of humanity is making and confesses itself bound to make?

I think that the imperative of the individual conscience, corrected by such inquiry, will give us an approximate rule of right conduct. And such rule will tend to become more and more nearly perfect as the progress which the conscience of humanity is making, and the nature of the command in obedience to which it is made, are more clearly manifested in detail.

(12.) Can we get any help toward the perfecting of this approximate rule from the observed relation of pleasure and pain to righteousness? Certainly not, if we look to details. Take any action in particular, and we may say that the pleasure or pain which attends it is not in any appreciable degree even presumptive evidence that it is right or that it is wrong. But suppose we had reason to believe that on the whole and in the long run the happiness of humanity would increase in proportion to its righteousness, might we not then say that such kind of action as had in the long lapse of past ages tended on the whole to increase the happiness of humanity was presumably the right conduct? Surely we might. And we should in that case have an important help towards the perfecting of our approximate rule. If we (I.) set aside all calculation of consequences based upon the pleasure or pain which attends any particular action. If we (II.) inquire whether the result of such action will be in harmony with the progress which the conscience of humanity is making, and confesses itself bound to make. And if (III.) we inquire whether the result of such actions, on the whole and in the long run, has been conducive to the happiness of mankind, we shall have a rule of right conduct as nearly correct as natural religion can supply. And the longer the world lives and the fuller the knowledge that we acquire of the whole history of humanity, the more correct will such rule become.

But it is evident that the value of the last factor of the rule depends upon the answer to a question which has already several times suggested itself to us in the course of this inquiry. Is the universe, in fact, one, and is the principle of its unity favourable to righteousness? If either clause of this question be answered in the negative, then the tendency of actions to make men happy or miserable is no evidence at all of their quality as right or wrong. The solution of this question in its first clause will be attempted in the next chapter.

(13.) Meanwhile it may be stated here that in respect of the matter of the inquiry just concluded, revealed religion stands broadly distinguished from natural religion. Revealed religion, if it be recognized as revealed, implies a consciousness of being taught by God; and if it be recognized as religion, it implies a criterion of righteousness. It follows that revealed religion must offer to its disciple a criterion of righteousness recognized as divinely given. There might conceivably be a revelation which would present no such criterion: a revelation of knowledge of things beyond the limits of the range of our natural powers: a revelation to excite wonder or to satisfy some of our intellectual aspirations. But such a revelation would not be a revelation of religion. Religion implies a rule of conduct. No system can be put forward as a system of religion unless it contain such a rule.

Such a rule is inherent in Christianity. It is not merely given by Christianity or merely embodied in Christianity. We may not say: Given Christianity and Christianity will give you the rule, but, Given Christianity and you have the rule. For Christ is the essential fact of Christianity, and Christ Himself is the rule.

The Christian possesses a practical criterion whereby he can determine the order of precedence which he ought to assign to his various faculties in the endeavour to fulfil them in due harmony. That criterion is not a series of commandments and ordinances; it is a life. It is not an ideal merely; it is an ideal actually realized. This is the characteristic difference of Christianity. In this is to be found the key to its history, and on this converge also the main lines of evidence which establish its truth.

CHAPTER II.

(14.) Our inquiries up to this point have brought us face to face with these problems: Is the universe one? and, Is the principle of its unity favourable to righteousness? The consideration and criticism of the former of the two is the purpose of the present chapter.

The phrase, "The universe is one," may be said to be open to some objection. It looks like an identical proposition: the predicate seems to be implied in the subject. Or, if not, it may be said to be ambiguous. It will be well, therefore, before proceeding further, to define one's terms.

I mean, then, by the universe all objects of sense, mediate* and immediate, possible† and actual. And when I say that all these are one, I mean that they all form a single and coherent system which proceeds upon one principle and is subject to one law, insomuch that whatsoever is in the whole is in the principle from which the whole proceeds. I mean that all items of our knowledge of them, and all the symbols of our thoughts about them, are mutually interdependent, and stand in relation to one another through a single governing principle.

* Mediate, *e.g.*, atoms and ether.
† Possible, *e.g.*, animals (if any) in the planets.

(15.) It is clear that such a hypothesis as this is not capable of inductive proof. For, whatsoever the extent of our knowledge be, the possible extent of that which is for the present beyond our knowledge will be infinitely greater. A proof, if applied only to things within the actual range of our faculties, may reach a very high degree of certainty, and yet if we apply it to all things within the conceivable range of our faculties, it may dwindle to a very low degree of probability. Astronomers are very fully acquainted with the movements of the solar system. But the solar system is a mere point in the universe, and any argument based upon our knowledge of it would be, if applied to the whole universe, the "loosest" and most "uncertain" kind of "simple enumeration." Beyond the range of the solar system a star here and there may be shown to belong to a system in some respects analogous to the solar system. But the movements of the stars in general, as known to astronomers, are quite incoherent, and show scarce a trace of mutual relation. Some of them, indeed, are such as, in the present state of knowledge, to negative the possibility of such relation. One star, for example, is known to be moving at such a rate that the attraction of all the known bodies of the universe cannot stop it or even direct it.*

Yet I suppose that astronomers believe that the movements of the stars are somehow coherent, even

* 1830 Groombridge. Newcombe's "Popular Astronomy," p. 485 et seq.

though the ultimate principle of their coherence be yet unknown. And I suppose that every astronomer expects that such coherence will be one day proved, and its principle expounded, and the law of it stated. Indeed, I suppose that astronomers, if they could penetrate those regions of space which would still be beyond the range of the telescope if that range were a thousand times extended, would expect to find coherence and harmony prevailing there. And yet there is scarce a shadow of inductive proof to justify such a conclusion. And whatsoever shadow there is becomes not more distinct but less. If, indeed, the whole of the universe, or the greater part of it, lay anyhow within our ken, experience might give us a degree of confidence which would be ever on the increase. But the fact is that the more we extend the range of our knowledge, the more largely looms in proportion the region which is beyond our knowledge. Or put it this way : The range of the universe is infinite, and the range of our knowledge at any given time is finite. No proportion is possible between them. Experience, therefore, never can furnish any secure basis for a conclusion concerning the interaction and harmony of the various objects in the universe. And yet the astronomer, howsoever far he may be able to cast his plummet into the depths of space, expects to find order and harmony there in proportion to his knowledge. So strong a hold has " the expectation of likeness " on the human mind.

(16.) The expectation of likeness is, in fact, admitted

on all sides to be dictated by a law of the human mind. J. S. Mill* says: "I agree with Mr. Bain in the opinion that the resemblance of what we have not experienced to what we have, is, *by a law of our nature*, presumed through the mere energy of the idea before experience has proved it." What is it that the law of our nature presumes, and what is it that "experience" proves? Not the same thing, certainly. For the "law of our nature" presumes resemblance *ad infinitum*. Mill's language admits as much, for he says, "resemblance of what we have not experienced:" and if we attempt to sum up what we have not experienced, it is evident that we shall never get the sum done. But experience never can prove resemblance *ad infinitum*. That which we have not experienced must continue to be for ever infinitely more than what we have experienced.

It seems to follow that the ground of our belief in the uniformity of nature is psychological and not logical. It is a postulate which is given in the constitution of our minds. It is not the conclusion of an argument. Our nature compels us to presume in general that which in the nature of things is incapable of logical proof. And then, as each particular instance comes within the range of our experience, we have to verify the presumption in that particular case. For this reason above all, because we want to know not only that there is a resemblance,

---

* Mill's "Logic," p. 378, People's edition, 1884—note.

we want to know also what the resemblance is. And the psychological presumption only answers the former question. The logical process has to establish the latter. And no doubt the proof in each case of what the resemblance is will tend to confirm in the next case the expectation of resemblance. But no proof of resemblance in any finite number of cases can be accepted as a proof or even as presumption of resemblance in the whole number of cases, which is infinite.

(17.) The matter appears to stand thus : We start with the presumption that the facts which we have yet to learn will cohere somehow with the facts which we have already learned. As each new fact comes within our knowledge we ascertain by some sort of inquiry at what point and how it coheres with the facts which were within our knowledge before. By-and-by we begin to reflect upon the presumption with which we started, and we find that it has no limit. It is, in fact, a presumption that the whole universe is one coherent system which proceeds upon one principle. But no enumeration of particulars, howsoever systematic and howsoever carefully checked, can ever justify a presumption of that sort. We cannot scale the infinite by finite steps. Such a presumption can only be justified by showing that without it thought is impossible, and that every act of thought implies it. If we can show that, we shall have established its validity as a law of thought.

But before we try to show it we must first attempt

some further development of the presumption in question.

(18.) The presumption is that the universe forms a single and coherent system; that there is nothing "sporadic" in it; that there is a way to be found all through it, from any one part to every other part; that it so exists that wheresoever and whensoever any part of it is thoroughly explored, such part will be found to be in harmonious relation to every other part. We all assume that the world in which we find ourselves belongs to such a system. Every scientific inquiry into the unknown and undiscovered proceeds upon the assumption that it does. Scientific or unscientific, we all take this for granted, howsoever much we try not to take it for granted; and it seems as if we could not help taking it for granted. The assumption was latent in the thought or the *quasi*-thought of the first creature that made preparation for night or for winter. We made it unconsciously for untold ages. We have now for a long time made it consciously and deliberately. We have called it "the law of causation." We have wrangled about it, we have tried to prove it, and we have tried to prove that it couldn't be proved. But none of us has ever seriously doubted it. And it has always been justified by experience. Even the very phenomena which at one time seem to be inconsistent with it are at last found to justify it on a fuller scale, insomuch that such apparent inconsistencies are now always held to be the prelude to larger generalizations of it. What is the meaning of it?

(19.) The existence of any coherent collocation of things conditioning with absolute certainty a series of developments unrealized as yet, implies undoubtedly the presence of an idea. And a system of infinite extent, so conditioning every such series, implies the presence of an infinite idea. Such a system as we all assume the universe to be implies the presence of an idea controlling the universe in all its parts.

Some have attempted to build upon this law of causation an argument in favour of monotheism; and some contend that it will give no support at all to any such argument. The fact is that if the law of causation be anything short of an absolute and universal postulate of reason, it will furnish no proof at all of monotheism. And if it be such an absolute and universal postulate, it is not a proof but an expression of monotheism. If by "cause" we understand simply the antecedent indicated by experimental inquiry, formulated and tested by the laws of inductive logic, then cause never can become an absolute and universal principle. The field of experiment is always finite, and so can yield no conclusion which can govern the infinite. Cause in that case will give no proof of God. But if we understand by cause the unifying principle of the universe; that which conditions absolutely every series of actions and events; then cause does not prove God: cause is God.

(20.) We are now in a position to inquire, Can an absolute law of universal causation be established as a law of thought? If it can, then monotheism is a law of thought. For an absolute law of universal causation cannot be formulated without the implication of monotheism. The statement of monotheism and the statement of such a law are, in fact, identical propositions.

We have already learned that such a law cannot be established by inductive inquiry, because inductive inquiry can only yield conclusions which are valid in a finite field. Or put it thus: Every inductive inquiry starts with the assumption of the unity of nature within the field of the inquiry: if it contemplate a universal conclusion, it must contemplate an absolute unity of nature. It seems, therefore, that to seek to establish monotheism by a process of inductive inquiry is to reason in a circle; for such inquiry, directed to such an end, involves the assumption of an absolute law of universal causation, and such a law implies monotheism.

(21.) What, then, becomes of the argument from design, for that is an inductive argument? No doubt the argument from design is highly important and, within its limits, conclusive. And, as I shall try to show in the next chapter, its importance and conclusiveness are not weakened but enhanced by the doctrine of evolution. J. S. Mill, I think, in that single particular, extenuates the argument unfairly. But I think that he very fairly estimates the conclusion which, standing by itself, it results in. Intelligence is a condition precedent of the world of which we have experience. And there is a strong presumption that the Maker of the world desires the happiness of His creatures, although it would appear that there is something else that He desires even more. That, I think, is the net result of the argument from design. It is a very important result, and, I think, an inexpugnable result. But it certainly does not amount to monotheism. For if it should be supposed that the intelligence which is a condition precedent of the world in which we dwell is one of many co-ordinate intelligences, each ruling a different region; or even that such intelligence is in conflict with such other intelligences; the argument from design does not disprove such hypothesis, but even offers one or two considerations which might be thought to strengthen it. For monotheism, I repeat, is an absolutely universal proposition, and the argument from design is an inductive argument, and it is against the nature of such an argument to establish such a proposition.

(22.) Monotheism may, nevertheless, be established as a necessary postulate of thought.

Every state of consciousness implies a standard in virtue of its correspondence with which it is valid. For example, I perceive certain objects to be blue in colour, other objects green, and others red. Another man perceives the same objects, but to him they are all red or blue. My blues and greens are all one colour to him; he sees two colours where I see three. Which of us is right? Differences of a similar sort may exist in every direction, and there is absolutely nothing to prove that the world presents the same aspect to any two creatures. We agree to give the same name to an object, and the very fact that we give it the same name hides from us the difference of our perceptions of it, if such difference there be. I and another agree to call the same thing green, and we may never perhaps find out that my green is not the same as his green. Only if one of us sees three colours to the other's two is there much chance of such discovery.

Which of us is right, and which of us is wrong?

(23.) Suppose it be said, Any sensation of colour is nothing but the result of certain physical movements, some within the body and some beyond it; if any of these differ in different cases, the result of them, of course, in each case differs too. Then it may be said in reply: Granted that certain physical movements are the antecedents, and, as far as we know, the invariable antecedents, of the sense of colour; still it remains true that my sense of colour or yours represents or else does not represent a fact. If it does not represent a fact, then the sense of colour is nothing but an illusion, and truth in respect of it is nothing but what any man troweth; and so in respect of every other sense. If it represent a fact, does it represent it truly? Two mutually exclusive representations of the same fact cannot be true. Blue and not blue are mutually exclusive. If it represent a fact there must be a standard in virtue of its agreement with which the representation is valid. What is that standard?

(24.) Perhaps the objector may still demur. He may say: It is true that the sense of colour represents a fact, but it represents in each case a different fact. The fact in each case is the sum of physical movements, vibratory or whatsoever else, within the body and without it. These are different in your case and in mine, and so the colour which represents them is, of course, different; there is no contradiction. But it may be said in reply that, whatosever reason there be for believing that the sense of colour has an invariable antecedent in certain physical movements, there is the same reason for believing that such physical movements have an invariable antecedent in the nature and constitution of the object. How is it, then, that the same object, without any change of nature or constitution, is of a different colour to your consciousness and mine? And suppose that the objector should reply: Because the object expresses itself in a different language to you and to me: in the language of my consciousness it is red, in the language of your consciousness it is blue; the statement is the same in each case, only made in a different language. The answer is (I.) that the analogy is a false one. The language is the same in each case; we both describe the object in the language of colour. It is the statement of the fact which is different. I call it red and you call it blue. Besides (II.) it sometimes happens that one of us sees a difference and the other sees no difference at all. We both see a number of objects: to me some of them are green and some of them are blue; to you they are all brown. The analogy of language will give the objector in this case no show of help at all. If I give in my language two differing descriptions of two objects, and if you in your language describe them both by the same words, one of us must be wrong. The astronomers tell us that the red stars and the white stars are each in a different stage of development. But suppose the stars appear to me some red and some white, and all white to you, then my consciousness tells me of the difference and yours does not. Which of us is right, and which of us is wrong?

(25.) It is certain that it will not do to say that the majority is right and the minority wrong. If all the world but one man says that black is white, the one man is right and the world wrong. My perception of colour is relative to me, but it is relative also to something which is not me. What is that something? The question must be answered. Every rational creature believes, and cannot but believe, that the colour which he sees, say in a particular star, has reference to something which existed before he was born, and which will continue to exist after he is dead. The colour of the star is determined by facts which are independent of him and of all men. There is a standard somewhere to which his perception must correspond, and only in virtue of its correspondence with such standard is it a true perception. What is that standard?

(26.) Shall we say that it is the thing in itself as perceived neither by us nor by any other? Hardly, for all facts of which we are or can be cognizant resolve themselves in the last analysis into states of consciousness, and so a thing which is not at all perceived, even if potentially something, is actually nothing. To set up the thing in itself as a standard is as good as to say that there is no standard. Still we know that men's consciousness of the same thing often differs, and may differ more than we know. Must we admit, then, that there is no question of either the truth or the falsehood of any such facts of consciousness, even if they be contradictory?

(27.) Such an admission would amount to a denial of the possibility of all systematic thought, and the intellect rejects it as absurd. We must revert to the thing-in-itself, but we must reject the definition of it which equates it with nothing. The thing-in-itself, if it is to be a thing at all, must be a state of consciousness; not of your consciousness, nor of mine, nor of any particular consciousness whatsoever: it must be a state of a consciousness which is universal. It is only in virtue of its correspondence with the fact as it exists for the universal consciousness that any particular consciousness of a fact is valid. Either there is a universal consciousness to which every particular consciousness is related and subordinate, or else all our perceptions and thoughts are without any real validity or coherence, and the world in which we find ourselves is but a mere play of dream-shadows.

(28.) It was impossible that this argument could appear in a fully developed form until the analysis had been completed which resolves all our knowledge into states of consciousness. Nevertheless the germ of it appears in Plato, and it may be seen, although in hardly a more advanced stage, in philosophers of later date, notably in Bruno and Malebranche.

In Berkeley it begins to assume a decisive shape. It became obscured for Kant on account of his hesitating and unsatisfactory doctrine of "things-in-themselves." It seems as if by Kant "things-in-themselves" are made to usurp the place of the universal consciousness. And, in consequence, the universal consciousness is not for him a postulate of the speculative reason. His disproof of what he calls material and dogmatic idealism amounts to this;* that the *"ego"* of consciousness implies a universal *non ego*. But it implies this only because, as we have seen, it implies a universal consciousness not mine. Nothing but his doctrine of things-in-themselves hindered Kant's refutation of idealism from becoming a speculative proof of monotheism. Kant's philosophy is, no doubt, a "possession for ever," but it needed the researches of his great successors to deliver it from the confusion imparted to it by his doctrine of "things-in-themselves." Things-in-themselves, in so

* "Critique of Pure Reason: Transcendental Analytic," book ii., chap. ii., section 4.

far as they differ from things as perceived by us, can only be things as they exist in the universal consciousness. And only in virtue of its agreement with this consciousness, is your consciousness or mine, or any man's, true or valid.

(29.) This doctrine, in its fully developed form, has been made by T. R. Green the foundation of his ethical philosophy. Green's position stands in contrast with the position of Kant. Kant argues from morals to God. To him the thing given is the imperative of conscience, and from this he infers the existence of God as a postulate of the practical reason. For Green, on the other hand, the consciousness of God is implied in every single act of consciousness of you or me. There is a progressive effort of the individual consciousness to realize its unity with the consciousness of God. And out of this effort the moral idea by degrees emerges.

The two views stand in contrast, but the affirmative part of both may be held together. The datum of Kant is the moral idea. The datum of Green is the existence of God. And both data stand in such relation to one another that from either the other can be inferred. From the moral idea we may infer the existence of God, and from the existence of God we may infer the moral idea. And it is of great importance that we should be able to accept both of these data, and that, while we apprehend rightly the relationship in which they stand, we should not leave either to be inferred from the other. If they both stand for us, each on an independent basis of its own, they will support one another, and so enhance the fulness alike of our speculative and practical convictions.

(30.) There is at present a tendency in some quarters to separate ethics from religion. Professor Huxley, if I recollect rightly the purport of one of his latest fugitive papers, thinks it highly desirable that they should be so separated. The hypothesis that there is no relation between them, or even that they are antagonistic, is *prima facie* possible. But I think such hypothesis, on closer examination, loses all probability, and ultimately destroys itself. The power which is manifested in the universe, if in theory we divest it of moral purpose, becomes more and more for us

" A power as of the gods gone blind,
Who see not what they do."

And ethical philosophy, if we deny God, tends to sink into a cunningly calculated search for pleasure or a perpetually shifting fashion, or, at the best, to rise into a sort of empty defiance of an impersonal and unconscious, but unconquerable fate. But if we recognize a power behind nature, and if we attribute to such power, if not personality, yet "something higher," and if, at the same time, we recognize a moral obligation, and a progress in nature favourable to the fulfilment of a high moral purpose, we can hardly fail to refer to the power both purpose and obligation. Or, if we ourselves fail to take this final and decisive step, our disciples will take it for us, as Mr. Fiske has done for Mr. Herbert Spencer.

(31.) If we do not recognize the imperative of conscience, both as manifested in the individual and in the race, we have no means of determining what God's will is except by a process of observation and experiment extending over a series of ages; observation and experiment with a view to the solution of this question: What sort of action tends, upon the whole, to elevate and strengthen mankind. On the other hand, if we do not recognize a power behind nature which is personal or more than personal, we have no means of correcting our interpretation of the imperative of conscience, and our impulse to obey it, although far nobler than the suicide's, will often be as blind and as desperate as his. Without the combination of both beliefs, natural religion can scarcely discover any practicable rule of righteousness. Out of such combination a rule arises, as we have seen, which supplies at least a general principle for the guidance of our conduct, and which for ever approaches, though it never attain, perfection.

(32.) My purpose in the present chapter has been to prove that the constitution of our minds requires us to admit monotheism as a postulate of thought. It may, perhaps, be urged that you do not prove a fact by proving that it must be taken for granted. The point, if it be worth insisting on, may be admitted. What you do prove is that if the fact be not admitted nothing at all can be known to be true. And this comes practically to the same thing; for, as an American philosopher has characteristically said, "The bank that refuses its own paper is hopelessly insolvent."

But I suppose that there will always be a few minds which will accept the alternative, which will deny all possibility of knowledge, and which will persist in regarding the universe as a conundrum that can only be given up.

And it must be admitted that the other alternative is of so absolute a character, so penetrating and so imposing, once it is understood, that one cannot wonder if the human mind hesitates before accepting it. For it means that the existence and presence of God are implied in every act, whether of sensation or of reflection. It means that if God be subtracted from the universe nothing remains; nothing, whether in *esse* or in *posse*. It means

> "That if the Nameless should withdraw from all
> Thy frailty counts most real, all thy world
> Would vanish like thy shadow in the dark."

(33.) In the absence of revelation, therefore, I am inclined to doubt if absolute monotheism would ever have been heartily accepted by any but a few. Those few, indeed, would, I doubt not, be more in number and much more in influence than those who would accept the only alternative, *i.e.*, the impossibility of all knowledge. The great majority of thinkers, and all others, would most likely attempt some illogical compromise. Natural religion without revelation would be always trying to limit the meaning of the universe. Men would come to believe in a multiplicity of "universes" governed by a multiplicity of conflicting intelligences. Or some other hypothesis would be adopted which would relieve men's minds from the persistent pressure of the infinite. The long survival and frequent recurrence of Manicheism is a noteworthy fact. The extent to which it has leavened Catholic Christianity is even more noteworthy, and the hold which kindred doctrines have obtained upon some philosophic minds is perhaps in this regard the most noteworthy fact of all. The great variety of dualistic systems which treat mind and matter as co-ordinate and distinct are all essentially opposed to the law of universal causation; a law which, as we have seen, implies monotheism and is implied by it. If everything in the universe proceeds from the one all-controlling idea, then matter must either be the representation of that idea by itself to itself, or else the self-imposed condition under which it is fulfilling itself. There can be no doubt, I think, that Christianity, by holding up monotheism to the human mind as the one fundamental truth, has greatly helped to determine philosophy in the direction of monism. And monism in philosophy has reacted, and is still reacting, as a witness to monotheism and as an interpreter of it.

CHAPTER III.

(34.) We have seen that an inductive argument is incapable of proving an absolutely universal proposition. But the argument from design is an inductive argument, and monotheism is an absolutely universal proposition. It follows that the argument from design is of no avail to prove absolute monotheism. Nevertheless it is of great value, for the conclusion which it yields, although by no means amounting to monotheism, is nevertheless one without which monotheism would have no practical meaning for us. An absolute and infinite being conditioning the universe in all its parts, but of which we cannot predicate intelligence, may indeed be an object of wonder. But I do not see how belief in such a being can yield us any rule of conduct. And a doctrine which yields no rule of conduct is, from the religious point of view, null. Now the argument from design tells us nothing at all about an absolute and infinite cause of the world, but it does tell us about an intelligent cause of the world. The laws of thought constrain us to postulate an absolute and infinite cause of all things whatsoever, and the argument from design enables us to attribute intelligence to the cause of all things that we know. And so the primary postulate of thought becomes the basis of religion.

(35.) I am aware, indeed, that the conclusion of the

argument from design was already implicit in the primary postulate of thought. The idea which conditions the sum of things, the universal consciousness which is implied in every particular consciousness is by the very terms of the statement, intelligent. But such intelligence is much more easily apprehended by us when shown in detail by the argument from design. As matter of history the force of the argument from design was well understood and appreciated before the primary postulate of thought was formulated, much more before such an analysis of thought was possible as would enable us to justify it. And this fact is, of itself, sufficient indication that the argument from design is more easily apprehensible by the average human mind.

(36.) There is a notable theory of modern science which has been held to invalidate the argument from design ; not, indeed, by setting aside any of the instances on which it is based, but by discovering a fact other than creative intelligence which will account for the circumstance which is common to them all. The theory in question seems to be not unlikely to secure for itself a place among the recognized laws of nature. It becomes necessary, therefore, to inquire what effect, if any, it will have, if so recognized, upon the argument from design.

It will help, I think, to clear the ground for such inquiry if I exhibit the argument in the first place as applied to establish a conclusion which has no direct bearing upon religion. I will then proceed to exhibit it as directed to the establishment of the conclusion that this world is the work of an intelligent Maker. We shall have before us then the objection to which I have referred, and we shall be in a position to inquire why it is made in one case and not in the other, and the inquiry will, I think, throw an instructive light upon the nature and value of the objection.

(37.) There have been discovered in many parts of the world certain broken pieces of flint, varying in size, varying in position, varying also greatly in the numbers of them which are found in any one place together, but all agreeing in this one circumstance, that they are fit for the purpose of cutting. The fact that they are all flint is not another circumstance in which they agree, it is part of this one circumstance, for the fact of their being flint helps to make them fit for cutting. The numbers of such flints discovered are so great that we cannot suppose their agreement in this one circumstance to be the result of chance. We conclude that this one circumstance is the cause, or else an indispensable part of the cause, of their existence in this form. But now the act of cutting does not precede, but follows the formation of the flint; so it cannot be the cutting, but the purpose or intention to cut, that was the true cause of the formation of the flint implement. But this means that it was made by an intelligent maker. Here is an inductive argument, conducted according to the " Method of Agreement," and it is an argument which has convinced men of science all over the world.

(38.) Now let us turn to the same argument as it is applied to the establishment of the conclusion that the manifold adjustments of nature are the work of an intelligent Maker. And of these adjustments let us take for example that one which J. S. Mill himself takes in his criticism of the argument.* Instead of the flint axes let us take the eyes of living creatures. And here the argument is even stronger than in the other case, for every eye is not only a single instance: it combines in itself such a number of instances as to exclude the hypothesis of chance. "All the parts of which the eye is composed," says Mill, "resemble one another in this very remarkable property that they all conduce to enabling the animal to see." The argument runs exactly as before. For the property of being fitted to cut with, we have the property of being fitted to see with. And we conclude as before that this property is the cause, or an indispensable part of the cause, of the formation of the eye. And then, just as in the former case, comes the sequel of the argument. Sight does not precede, but follow, the formation of the eye. It is not the fact of sight, therefore, but the purpose to make sight, which is the true cause of its formation. And this means that the eye is the work of an intelligent Maker. But then Mill says:—"This part of the argument is not so inexpugnable as the former part. Creative forethought is not absolutely the only link by which the

---

* "Essays on Religion," 3rd edition, p. 171.

origin of the wonderful mechanism of the eye may be connected with the fact of sight. There is another connecting link. . . . This is the principle of the '*survival of the fittest.*'"

Now let us apply this criticism to our first instance. For there, too, as in the other case, there is a "survival of the fittest." There would have been first a slab of broken flint, scarcely more fit for cutting than any stone that you might pick up upon the shore or the moor, and deriving that slight fitness perhaps from accident. And from that up to the best of the flint axes there would be a progressive improvement, perhaps by almost imperceptible degrees, perhaps by a few well-marked stages from less to greater fitness. Why should we not say: The forethought of the maker is not the only link by which the formation of the axe may be connected with the fitness to cut. "There is another link, the principle of the survival of the fittest." When the criticism is thus applied, we see at once that it is illogical and unfair. The "survival of the fittest" and the "forethought of the maker" are not only not exclusive of each other; they are not even contrasted alternatives. For the theory of the "forethought of the maker" is an account of origin, and the theory of the "survival of the fittest" is an account of process. Origin by the forethought of the maker is consistent with an infinite variety of process. And such a process as the survival of the fittest implies an origin by forethought of the maker. One does not say of the making of the statue :

We need not suppose that the sculptor designed it, for it may have been wrought by the graving tool and chisel. The survival of the fittest is a theory of the means whereby the forethought of the maker effects his design. And it implies, at the least, three things: (I.) the making of somewhat; (II.) the differentiation of the thing made into several things; and (III.) the adoption for the ultimate purpose of the best of these. The forethought of the maker is not by any means set aside, nor the evidence for it in any degree attenuated, by the principle of the survival of the fittest.

(39.) It is impossible to avoid the conclusion that the combinations and functions and symmetrical arrangement of the world in which we find ourselves were contrived by intelligence. When we consider the action and reaction, one upon another, of the various natural objects by which we are surrounded, and with which we are connected: the mechanism of the eye and ear, of the flower, of the blood-vessel, of the seed-vessel, all accurately adapted to special purposes; the adjustment of the earth upon its axis, and the consequent succession of the seasons; the mutual relation one to another of suns, planets, and moons, we are constrained by reason to attribute all this to intelligence: intelligence of the same sort as ours, but immeasurably beyond ours in power and invention and resource. And the more we analyze and systematize the reason which so constrains us, the more impossible we find it to escape from the constraint. Every hypothesis by which we endeavour to evade the conclusion succeeds only in shifting the place of the presiding intelligence. By one it seems to be thought an attribute of matter, by another of nature, as of an abstract entity. But you cannot think away the Maker by changing His name, or by trying to identify Him with His material.

(40.) Nor can you ignore Him by substituting process for origin. When you have shown how a thing grew, you have not in the least shown how it came into being. Growing implies an antecedent being made. A thing must be before it can grow. And the fact that it grew, or that it grew in this way or in that way, is no answer at all to the question how it came to be. Suppose we grant that the eye grew to its present perfection, or say to its present degree of excellence, from a rudimentary type: whence came that type, and how did it come to have capacity for improvement? The doctrine of the survival of the fittest, or of natural selection, or any other interpretation of the theory of evolution, may or may not be a very good account of how the Maker made the world, but it cannot be a substitute for the Maker. If the theory of evolution be true, and if the evidence of design in nature be conceived in accordance with it, that evidence becomes greatly enhanced both in force and scope. For then it comes to us not merely as exhibited once for all in an instrument such as the eye: nicely, but not with absolute perfection, adapted to its purpose. It comes to us rather as exhibited in a series of progressive works linked on one to another, each unfolding the hidden design more and more fully, and each by its improvement upon that which preceded it giving more and more assured promise of absolute perfection to come. The further you go back the more deeply you bury in obscurity the fulness of the design, but the more you enlarge its implicit grandeur. If the primal firemist of which the evolutionists tell us, contained within itself all the varied life and beauty of the present earth, then each new epoch in the history of the system and of the earth is a new revelation of the greatness of the design of Him who made the primal firemist. And not only so, but each such revelation is a fresh pledge of the magnificence, as yet unrevealed, of His design in its completeness.

(41.) It may be urged, perhaps, that so magnificent a design would be still more magnificent if it were to spring into fulfilment in a moment instead of gradually growing to fulfilment during an immeasurable series of ages. The answer to this is that what we call "time" is a condition attaching to our imperfect powers of apprehension. It consists in observed succession, and it exists therefore only for those who are incapable of seeing all things in one view, and whose states of consciousness are, for that reason, successive. Absolutely the design is already realized in its completeness. For its whole being consists in the states of consciousness of the designer, and those states of consciousness are co-existent, and not successive. As I think T. R. Green would have put it, the unifying consciousness, which is universal, and which is given in every single act of consciousness, is out of time. Or, as it was put long ago by one who did not aim at philosophical exactness of expression: "One day is with the Lord as a thousand years, and a thousand years as one day."

(42.) I am aware that this way of putting the matter brings us face to face with perhaps the most formidable problem in theology. How shall we identify the Absolute Being whom the laws of thought imply with the Maker of the world, in whom inductive reasoning constrains us to believe? The problem is very old and very new. Very old, and yet I do not find that it emerges in the Old Testament. The Hebrew, indeed, was amongst the earliest who recognized the Maker of the world. And whether early or late, he also recognized the Self-existent and Eternal One who is past finding out. But he seems not to have recognized the difficulty of identifying the one with the other. But the difficulty must have been recognized in the Oriental philosophies during Old Testament times. For as soon as ever Christianity and the Oriental philosophies came into contact, we find the attempt to distinguish between the Supreme Being and the Maker of the world beginning to be made. All the Gnostic heresies have this one point in common: they believe in the Supreme Being, and they believe in the Maker of the world, but they refuse to identify them. The Manichee, the descendant of the Gnostic, or say, rather, his cousin of a later generation, resembles him in this. And students of church history know how persistent this thought has been, and how it has clung to Christianity, and clings to it still, under all manner of strange disguises. All systems which assume nature to be inherently bad, or which attribute infinity to evil, base themselves, consciously or unconsciously, on the refusal to identify the Supreme Being with the Maker of the world.

(43.) But the problem is new as well as old. It appears in recent philosophies, which either ignore Christianity or else ostentatiously set it aside. Some of them recognize the Supreme Being, but refuse to recognize the Maker. I do not know whether in view of some of his latest utterances Mr. Herbert Spencer ought not to be called a theist, although I think it likely that he would still reject such a description of himself. And I do not know if J. S. Mill's theory of a probable Creator would entitle him to be called a theist. I should say not, if you define your terms exactly. But we may say of both of them that they are theists of a sort. Now, Mr. Herbert Spencer's God, if he has one, is the Supreme Being, and J. S. Mill's God is the Demiurge. Mr. Herbert Spencer says: "The power which transcends phenomena cannot be brought within the form of our finite thought, yet, as being a necessary datum of thought, belief in its existence has among our beliefs the highest validity of any." And again: "Amid the mysteries which become the more mysterious the more they are thought about, there will remain the one absolute certainty, that we are ever in the presence of an Infinite and Eternal Energy, from which all things proceed."* J. S. Mill says: "There is a large balance of probability in favour of creation by intelligence."† But Mill knows nothing of a Supreme Being, and Mr. Spencer knows nothing of a Maker of the world.

(44.) It is essential to catholic Christianity not only to recognize the Maker of the world and the first cause of all things, but further to recognize the fact that they are one. And it is not in the recognition of either, but in the identification of them, that the difficulty consists.

It is undoubtedly a very big difficulty: so big that if we find a solution of it we are sure to find such solution applicable more or less to all other speculative difficulties. I proceed to state it.

All arguments which constrain us to recognize the Maker, show Him to us working under limitations which appear strictly to condition His action. It is the very existence of the limitation which enables us to recognize Him. Contrivance is the basis on which the argument from design is founded. And contrivance implies limitation.

But the law which constrains us to recognize the supreme cause rejects the notion of limitation. The unity which we expect is a unity which pervades the

* "Nineteenth Century," 1884.
† "Essays on Religion," 3rd edition, p. 174.

universe. Thought refuses to set up a limit or to recognize a limit where the unifying power ceases to work. Thought finds it impossible, in the last resort, to recognize the existence of anything whatsoever except in dependence on the intelligence of the unifying power which fills the universe. Not to exist for that intelligence is not to exist at all.

How, then, shall we identify this absolute cause of all things with the Maker of the world? Is the proposition that they are identical self-contradictory? Certainly not; for it is evident that if we know the first cause at all, we must know Him under conditions. To say that we know Him is to say that He has come under conditions. I admit that we neither have nor can have any unconditional knowledge of Him. To say that we have, or can have, such knowledge is to make a self-contradictory statement. Nevertheless He is the object of our knowledge. Even Mr. Herbert Spencer admits that we are conscious of Him; for he speaks of "our consciousness of the unconditioned." But to say that we become conscious of the unconditioned is to say that the unconditioned becomes subject to conditions. And this Mr. Spencer also admits, for he speaks of the "undifferentiated substance of consciousness which is conditioned anew in every thought."* So there is no necessary contradiction in saying that the Maker of the world is the absolute

---

* "First Principles," chap. iv., 26.

cause of all things. For although the absolute cause of all things is in Himself by His very nature above all conditions, yet we may see Him as the Maker working under conditions.

(45.) But, if so, the conditions must be self-imposed. For everything which exists depends absolutely for its existence on Himself. And so the conditions which limit Him, whatsoever they be, material or moral, exist and continue to exist only in virtue of His own action. We may, without self-contradiction, adopt the hypothesis that the Maker of the world is no other than the Absolute First Cause of all things, provided we suppose further that He is acting as the Maker of the world under self-imposed conditions.

If we adopt the hypothesis with such proviso, we find ourselves immediately face to face with the question : Why does the Infinite Being submit Himself to conditions? And, indeed, we cannot evade this question in any case. For if we do not identify the Maker of the world with the Absolute First Cause we shall have to suppose another Maker of a higher order, and another still, and yet another, and so on through an infinite series. And such a hypothesis would still call for a solution of the question : Why does the Infinite Being submit Himself to limitations? We may, indeed, refuse to admit the existence of a universal consciousness. But, as I have shown above,* the outcome of such refusal is mere philo-

---

* Chap. ii., sec. 32, p. 42.

sophic nihilism. For the universal consciousness is a condition of the existence of all things. I think, therefore, that not only catholic orthodoxy but philosophy is bound to look for an answer to the question, Why does the Infinite Being impose limits upon Himself?

(46.) There are certain considerations which are suggested by analogy which may serve to show us the direction in which we ought to look for the answer. We observe that there are cases in which limitation enhances force. We may go further; for although it would not be true to say that limitation sometimes creates force, it is undoubtedly true to say that limitation is in some cases a condition *sine qua non* of the production of new forms of force. If a man means to do a great work he begins by imposing limits upon himself. What is art if it is not work done under difficult and rigorous conditions? What is civilization but the life of man reduced to conditions which limit it in order to enhance it? Why does a small but well-drilled army put to flight ten times its number of undisciplined and undrilled men? Because the army is acting under conditions. When Homer was about to tell the story of the wrath of Achilles, or of the wanderings of Ulysses, he might have told either if he would without submitting himself to the difficult and complex conditions of poetical composition. Had he done so he might have amused a few thousands of his companions and their children. But he submitted himself to those conditions, and so his work lives on still, to the delight and instruction of mankind.

I do not pretend to found a conclusion upon these analogies, but I do propose to found an inquiry upon them. Can we point to anything of which we may say these two things: (I) that it is the result of the self-limitation of the Creator, and (II.) that it is a thing so great that it is reasonable to assign it as the purpose of such self-limitation.

(47.) It will perhaps be thought that it may be affirmed of all phenomena whatsoever, that they imply the self-limitation of the Creator as the condition precedent of their existence. But this is not so. It is the essence of all phenomena that the universal consciousness perceives them: they exist for Him. But they do not limit Him: they are nothing but the action of His intelligence. "Thou takest away *their* breath, they die, and return to dust. Thou sendest forth *Thy* breath, they are created; and Thou renewest the face of the earth."* Is it true then, after all, that contrivance implies limitation? If all phenomena be nothing but the acts of the Supreme Intelligence, and if He act this way or that way as He pleases, must we say that He limits Himself if His acts appear as contrived? Certainly we must. For, if all things be nothing but the manifestation of God's thoughts, then contrivance is this, that God's thoughts are so ordered that (as Kepler said) others think them after Him.

---

* Psalm civ. 29, 30.

Contrivance implies the existence of self-conscious intelligences other than the Supreme Intelligence. And so contrivance implies limitation.

All phenomena, then, do not of necessity imply limitation of the Supreme Cause, but the existence of self-conscious intelligences does imply such limitation.

(48.) Can we find in the mere existence of subordinate self-conscious intelligences an adequate motive for the self-limitation of the Supreme? Is the self-conscious intelligence a self-determining intelligence? Or put it thus: Does self-consciousness imply self-determination? I am not concerned here to say that it does or that it does not. But I am concerned to say that if it does not it discloses no adequate motive for the self-limitation of the Supreme.

But it is evident enough that the Supreme has put upon Himself further limits than those which are implied in the mere existence of other self-conscious intelligences. One sort of limit is this: one must so act that others may trace his action. Another sort of limit is this: one so acts that others may resist one's action. Now, God has imposed upon Himself, not only the former sort of limit, but the latter. For whether or not self-consciousness implies self-determination, there are self-conscious intelligences who are also self-determining intelligences. Self-determination is a primary fact of our consciousness The ultimate meaning of this fact, and the real issue of the arguments which are supposed to invalidate it, I will consider in the next chapter. For the present

I assume it. Can we find, then, in the existence of self-conscious and self-determining intelligences an adequate motive for the self-limitation of the Supreme?

(49.) At first sight the problem seems to be rather complicated than solved. For all that we call moral evil springs out of the existence of self-determining intelligences, and the presence of moral evil in the world is the hardest part of the problem. How should God call into being powers who can, if they will, exert themselves for evil; some of whom have exerted themselves for evil, which evil God foresaw?

But what if God's purpose in calling such powers into being were to create virtue? There is no virtue without freedom, and freedom implies possible vice. To say that God could if He would make virtue without freedom, is the same sort of thing as to say that God could if He would make a triangle with only two sides. And that is to speak neither truly nor falsely; it is to talk nonsense. And suppose it be said that God, if He be good, would not call into being self-determining creatures if He saw that by their power of self-determination evil and not good would prevail, the answer is, Who says that He would or that He did? The more sure we are that God is good, the more sure we are that good and not evil will prevail, and the more sure we are also that, as we say, God foresaw such prevalence before He called any self-determining power into being; or, to speak more exactly, the more sure we are that such prevalence of good over evil is ever present to the eternal and universal consciousness. What if the whole history of creation be the history of a work whose final cause is morality? What if God made the world for the glory and beauty of goodness: what if he made the world in order to reproduce in the many the image of the Eternal One; the life

> "Which lives by law
> Acting the law it lives by,"

the spiritual freedom which knows no bond to be bound by except the love of God, and which

> "So bound is freest?"

Here we have an adequate motive for the self-limitation of the Supreme. Here we have the beginning of the final stage of that progress which has lasted throughout the ages ever since the first speck of life appeared on this or any other world, ever since matter took form and motion, ever since the first creative act of God. That progress has issued at last in the conscious endeavour to realize the beauty of goodness, to live by law, to offer to God the service which is perfect freedom.

(50.) I say the beginning of the final stage. For we may trace three distinct yet related stages of limitation imposed by the Creator upon Himself. The first stage of limitation is exhibited in that kind of action which so manifests itself that others, if there be others, may follow it step by step. This kind of action is throughout subjective; but the actor contemplates throughout the possibility of objective action. This kind of action we call "matter," and we trace it from the simplest interchange of position between the minutest particles to the most complicated movements of the non-sentient cosmos. After the cosmos has become sentient it still continues, but it is no longer the primary characteristic. While it lasts the limit imposed by the Creator upon Himself implies the possibility of disorder.

(51.) The second stage of limitation is exhibited in that kind of action which so manifests itself as to be reflexive. It brings into existence what in the former stage was always contemplated as possible; a subject other than the Creator, to whom the action of the Creator may be an object. This kind of action we call, in the abstract, "organic life," and we trace it from the lowest sentient thing to the highest intelligence which is not self-determining. After intelligence has become self-determining it still appears, but it is no longer the primary characteristic. It is distinguished throughout by that mutual relation between Creator and creature which produces in the creature the disposition which has been called "the expectation of likeness," a disposition which can be traced very low down indeed in the scale of living creatures, and which is the *sine qua non* of intellectual progress. While this second stage of limitation lasts the limit imposed by the Creator upon Himself implies the possibility of pain.

(52.) The third stage of limitation is exhibited in that kind of action which makes resistance to the actor possible. This kind of action creates freedom ; it calls into being self-determining creatures, who, if they obey God, must obey Him of their own will. The disposition which in the lower stage appeared as "expectation of likeness" appears as recognition of law, and becomes a *sine qua non* of moral progress. While this stage lasts, the limit imposed by the Creator upon Himself implies the possibility of sin.

Thus the whole course of the self-limitation of God is traceable through three stages, which are successive, but at last co-existent. And these three, although distinct, are all related, the later in each case implying the earlier. And so the purpose of the last is the purpose of the whole. And virtue is the purpose of the last.

But virtue, *i.e.*, righteousness, is the willing effort of each man to fulfil that command which the conscience of humanity recognizes, and acknowledges that it is bound to obey ; a command which prescribes a progress upward from brutality, a progress towards a state which is still undefinable, but the characteristics of which, each effort onward is tending to reveal more fully. They who are making such effort are the sons of God, and in them the image of God is reproduced. The manifestation of such, therefore, is the purpose for which all creation waits. It is the final cause of the self-limitation of the Supreme.

But it is evident that we must retrace our steps a little, for we have assumed here the answer to a question which still remains to be examined. We have learned that the whole system of things in which we find ourselves implies an idea co-extensive with itself: the universe implies an absolute power which controls it. But is this absolute power in harmony with the conscience of humanity? If He be, then we are entitled to conclude that the unconditional imperative which the conscience of humanity recognizes comes from Him: that His will is that principle transcending humanity which is implied in that imperative; and that perfect and voluntary fulfilment of that will by us is the goal beyond humanity which the conscience of humanity is endeavouring to attain to. But is He? Is the idea which is co-extensive with the whole system of things in harmony with the command which the conscience of humanity recognizes and acknowledges that it is bound to obey? Is the power which controls the universe a power which "makes for righteousness?" In short, is God good? With the examination of this question my task will be at an end. For the answer which I am prepared to give will be expressly dependent on the two great propositions which it is the purpose of revelation to state and justify; and my purpose here is not to write an exposition of revealed religion, but an introduction to the study of it.

CHAPTER IV.

(54.) WE have learned* that natural religion gives us no absolute rule of conduct, but that it does give us an approximate rule. Such rule is attained : (I.) By setting aside all consideration of any pleasure or pain to the actor himself which may result from any action. (II.) By inquiring if the results of such action as the unconditional imperative of the individual conscience seems to command are in harmony with the progress which the conscience of humanity is making and confesses itself bound to make. And (III.) by inquiring further if the result of the like actions have been on the whole and in the long run conducive to the happiness of mankind.

Conscience, whether of the individual or of the race, belongs to the continuing element of humanity which we know as personality, and it is therefore in itself independent of time. But it has to be interpreted by the individual in time. And the interpretation of conscience which each man has to make for himself, even if it were liable to error for no other cause, would be so liable for this cause. And of all the errors to which conscience is liable, the only corrective attainable by natural religion is the rule here stated. That

---

* Chap. i., sec. 12, p. 22.

rule, it will be observed, depends for its effectiveness on the comparison of a series of results; the fuller the series the better. And inasmuch as the results which may be so compared are always increasing in number, it follows that the ideal of good which is dictated by natural religion is never perfect, but is for ever approaching perfection.

(55.) The approximate rule by which we attain to this ideal depends, however, for its validity on the assumptions (I.) that the universe is one, and (II.) that the principle of its unity is favourable to righteousness. The first of these assumptions may receive theological or philosophical expression. If we give it philosophical expression we call it the doctrine of universal causation; if we give it theological expression we say that there is one God. This doctrine is incapable of proof by inductive methods, because it is an absolutely universal proposition. But it proves to be implicit in every act of thought and to be the primary datum of all reasoning. We can, therefore, have no higher certainty of anything than we have of it.

The second of these assumptions is closely related to the first; so closely that, unless we make it, the first, although all our knowledge depends upon it, seems to fade into the mere assertion of a transcendent somewhat which has no definite relation to thought. For we may prove by the methods of inductive reasoning that there is an intelligent Maker of the World, and it is a demand of natural religion that we should identify the Maker of the World with the Supreme Being, whose existence is implied in every act of thought. But such identification assumes that the Supreme Cause of all things is working under self-imposed limitations. And, therefore, an adequate motive of such self-limitation is a desideratum of natural religion. And such adequate motive may be found in morality; for morality implies the free agency of the individual, and the free agency of the individual implies the self-limitation of the Supreme.

But this account of the matter depends for its validity on the second assumption, namely, that the power which is manifested in the universe is favourable to righteousness; in other words, that the conscience of humanity is ultimately in harmony with the will of God; in short, that God is good. If God is not good we have no means of knowing whether or not the Maker of the World is God or some being less than God. If God is not good we have no means of knowing whether there is any relation whatsoever between Him and ourselves. If God is not good there is no means of bringing the individual interpretation of conscience into nearer agreement with an absolute standard. If God is not good we shall for ever suffer for virtue, and we shall never know surely that it is for virtue that we are suffering; truly, "if the Rulers of the Universe prefer the unjust man to the just man, it is better to die than to live." The question, therefore, "Is God good?" is of the very highest importance.

(56.) But before we inquire what reason may have to say to this question, there is a preliminary point to be settled. When we try to argue about morality, we must try to make sure first that we are not "beating the air." If there is no freedom there is no morality. And the doctrine of necessity, always logically strong, has been supposed to derive a decisive accession of strength from the doctrine of evolution. And, no doubt, if what we call moral phenomena are fully accounted for by the doctrine of evolution, the meaning of the word "moral" becomes wholly changed. If everything that we think or do is the certain result of antecedent forces over which we have had no control, then there is no such thing as moral freedom, and therefore that which we have assigned as an adequate motive for the self-limitation of the Supreme has, in fact, no existence.

And why not admit at once the conclusion that all things whatsoever, including our own acts and thoughts, are the certain result of antecedent forces over which we neither have nor ever had any control. The doctrine, as I have said, is logically strong, and fits in well with the doctrine of evolution. Besides, by accepting it we get rid of a formidable difficulty. The self-determining power of the creature is the one decisive evidence of that self-limitation which we are trying to understand. If we set aside self-determination, and if we reserve the question whether the consciousness which is at once object and subject implies it, we may say that all phenomena, whether mental or physical, are merely modes of the universal consciousness. Suppose we accept the doctrine that self-determination is a figment and illusion, the baffling elements which we call freedom and virtue disappear. It is true that the degree of the self-limitation of the Supreme which is indicated by the appearance of " contrivance" in the universe remains to be accounted for. But even if we do not see our way to dispose of contrivance as we have disposed of self-determination, the problem is greatly simplified. Why, then, should we not accept frankly the conclusion that self-determination is a figment?

Because we have certain elementary convictions which are to us the most certain of all things, and with which all our knowledge must ultimately correspond or else be practically worthless. If any apparent conclusion of reason contradicts these elementary convictions it destroys itself by so doing. If there be something which is not believable except at the cost of my capacity for believing anything, then it is to me absolutely unbelievable. If any philosophy, for example, in other respects perfect and admirable, involves the conclusion, say, that we ourselves have no real existence,

> " That nothing is, but all things seem,
> And we the shadows of a dream,"

then such philosophy is essentially incredible; for our own existence is that of which we have the highest certainty, and if we do not believe that we cannot believe anything at all. You cannot raise the level of a river higher than the source from which it flows. But the sense of personal freedom, limited, but real, is part of this given basis of our knowledge. (I know that in certain cases alternative courses are open to me, and I know that my volition "counts for something" in determining which course I shall take. I know that I can choose, and that I do choose, between this and that, and I know that I am responsible for my choice. If you take that knowledge away from me, you take away my power of knowing anything at all.) We reject the doctrine of necessity, and all which involves the doctrine of necessity, because it is contradictory of that which underlies all our knowledge, and such contradiction is fundamentally incredible.

(57.) But what about the logical argument and the accession of strength which it is supposed to derive from the doctrine of evolution? That we shall consider presently, but meantime we may observe that it is part of the first duty of an argument not to cut its own throat, and if it does cut its own throat the best thing that we can do is to bury its dead body and do the best we can without it. Still, if anyone be satisfied with the dead body of a self-slain argument, if anyone be willing to substitute for reason itself an art of reasoning which has parted with reason, he will find much advantage in "determinism." If one's object be simply to make a perfect system, a system that shall have no irregular angles or excrescences about it, he will be glad to be freed of an irrepressible and unmanageable element such as "free-will." But if one's object be to ascertain and understand facts, and not merely to make theories, one must be careful not to ignore free-will. To ignore free-will because it will not fit in with a theory, be that theory never so perfect and so admirable, is to sacrifice to theory that on which all theories must rest, and so in a different sense from the poet's,

"Propter vitam vivendi perdere causas."

For surely he who denies that volition and choice have any real existence belies the fundamental consciousness of mankind. If a philosopher ask me to believe that my own existence is a mere illusion, he makes no severer or more extravagant demand of me than if he ask me to believe that my free volition "counts for nothing" in the determination of my conduct. In either case he asks me to refuse to believe that of which I cannot help being absolutely certain. In either case he asks me to refuse to believe that which I am bound to assume every day and hour of my life. The existence of society, even the very existence of humanity, depends upon the assumption by ourselves that we are free. If we all agree to act upon the principle that nobody is responsible for his actions, we shall presently dissolve society, and with the dissolution of society all that is distinctive of humanity must perish. Everybody will remember with what humorous force Butler argues, not indeed that the doctrine of necessity is false, but that if it be true it must be true in some transcendental sense, which can have no relation at all to practice.

We have to remember, further, that one of the most valuable aids to the correction and enlargement of theories is to be found in what they call "residual phenomena." Some substance at the close of some carefully-conducted process refuses to behave as by the theory it ought to behave, or persists in appearing where by the theory it ought not to appear. Such refusal or persistence is a "residual phenomenon." Free-will is the residual phenomenon of the theory of evolution. It ought to disappear, and it refuses to disappear. Evolution is, perhaps, the grandest of modern speculations. Within the limits which it fairly covers, its importance can hardly be exaggerated. But it does not cover everything. It gives no account at all of the origin of things, and its account of moral phenomena, if it be applied to explain them, is in some respects contrary to fact.

(58.) And now we are in a position to examine the logical argument of the determinists. This, like every act of reasoning, rests ultimately on the doctrine that the universe is one. That means, as we have seen, that all objects of sense whatsoever, mediate or immediate,* possible or actual, belong to a single and coherent system, every part of which is in harmonious relation to every other part. According to this doctrine the universe, at any moment of time, may be

---

* Chap. ii., sec. 14, p. 25.

defined as a coherent collocation of things, conditioning with absolute certainty the whole series of yet unrealized developments. This doctrine is coming to be more and more unreservedly accepted, and certainly the theory of evolution tends greatly to its illustration and establishment. And in such a system as this doctrine contemplates, there is clearly no room for free-will.

But then such a system, a system of infinite extent absolutely conditioning the whole series of things to come, implies, as we have seen, an idea co-existent with itself.* Here is the obverse of the medal: You have the controlling idea and the controlled system of things. If there is no room for free-will on the one side, there is room for nothing else on the other; the one is the determined, the other is the determining. And if the free-will of man cannot be part of the controlled system, then it must be part of the controlling idea.

(59.) It is curious to observe how nearly the most opposite schools of thought are in agreement here. One tells us that freedom is not of the phenomenal, but of the noumenal world; that "the rational being can justly say of every unlawful action that he performs that he could very well have left it undone, because it, with all the past which determines it, belongs to the one single phenomenon of the character which he makes for

---

* Chap. ii., sec. 19, p. 31.

himself." * Another tells us that "we have an indefinite consciousness of an absolute reality transcending relations, which is produced by the absolute persistence in us of something which survives all changes of relation." And the same one speaks further of "the personality of which each is conscious, and of which the existence is to each a fact beyond all others the most certain." † And of this he says that "it cannot be truly known at all," although, himself being witness, we know that it is, and that it is the personality of each, and that it is unconditional. Yet another teaches that "quite apart from the sense in which all facts and events, including those of our natural life, are determined by that mind without which nature would not be, there is another sense in which we ourselves are not so much determined by it as identified by it with itself, or made the subjects of its self-communication." And again, "While the processes organic to the human consciousness are determined by the mind, to which all things are relative, in the sense that they are part of a universe which it renders possible, this consciousness itself is a reproduction of that mind, in respect, at least, of its attributes of self-origination and unification of the manifold." ‡

All these philosophers appear to mean that the self-conscious personality of man is independent of nature

---

* Kant, "Analytic of Pure Practical Reason" (Abbot's translation of Kant's Ethical Works), chap. iii., p. 191.
† Herbert Spencer, "First Principles," chap. iii., sec. 20.
‡ T. R. Green, "Prolegomena to Ethics," p. 82.

and of time, and belongs, in its essence, to the reality upon which all phenomena depend. And this, in fact, is the legitimate conclusion of the logic of the determinists. That logic certainly does prove that the self which is verily conscious in any degree of self-determining power, is, in so far, no part of the controlled system, but is, in so far, part of the controlling idea.

(60.) This result is in harmony with certain important results which are attained by other processes of reasoning. The organic structures which we call our bodies are part of the phenomenal world, and are determined, as the rest of nature is, by the controlling idea: they come into being, they change, and they die, in consequence of determinate antecedent conditions: they are apparently in a state of unceasing change; and although there is, no doubt, a sense in which they continue the same, it is impossible to say, from any outward study of them, what that sense is, or wherein that sameness consists. But we are conscious of a self which is not the body, although every act of which, as far as we know, that self is capable, implies a body. We are conscious that our self continues the same amidst all the changes of the body which come within our experience. And the self unifies for itself the perpetual series of sensations of which it is the subject, and which appear in all cases to imply some bodily change. This continuing self enables us to assign a meaning to the sameness which we cannot but attribute to the body, notwithstanding its changes of material. It is the same, inasmuch as it continues to be, as long as it lasts, organic to the same self. There is no other sense in which we can affirm it to be the same. But this inner sameness is manifested outwardly through the whole series of changes in the organism. A man's features are from first to last more or less clearly recognizable as the same features. And his body bears marks which continue as long as it continues. Which of these related facts, then, the self or the body, is the primary fact? Is it not reasonable to say that the self, which continues, is the first, and that the body, which is the same only in virtue of its being organic to the continuing self, is not the first, but the second. This result fits in well with the other. It is, in fact, the same result. The self is noumenal, and not phenomenal; it belongs to the continuing reality, not to the perpetually changing appearance. We see in it something of the power which organizes, and not merely the organic instrument. In other words, it belongs not to the controlled system, but to the controlling idea.

(61.) But the finite selves which limit the Supreme must be distinct from the Supreme. And yet they belong not to the controlled system, but to the controlling idea. It seems, then, that the self-limitation of the Supreme is wrought in the region which is not phenomenal. That otherness which He calls into existence is independent of all phenomena. And yet we learned above that the first stage of limitation imposed by the Creator upon Himself is matter, and the second organic life, and the third the free agency of the creature.* But this does not mean that the free agency of the creature is dependent on matter or organic life. It means that a certain time relation exists between them; and time, as far as I can see, is nothing but the succession of events, and where all events are contemplated in one view there is no time.

> "With the Nameless is nor day nor hour,
> Tho' we, thin minds, who creep from thought to thought,
> Break into 'thens' and 'whens' the Eternal Now."

Nevertheless the free agency of the creature implies both matter and organism. A thought must exist in order to be reflexive, and it must be reflexive in order to be self-determining. And that is the same as to say that, as contemplated in time, organic life precedes the free agency of the creature, and matter precedes organic life, for the material world is the thought of the Supreme conceived with reference to His purpose of self-limitation, and the organic world is that thought becoming reflexive, and the rational world is that reflexive thought become self-determining. And so, when we attempt to express the coming into existence, in time, of beings who are self-determining, we find ourselves constrained to assume the existence of matter and of organic life. "God formed man," we say, "of the ground, and breathed into his nostrils

---

* Chap. iii., sec. 50, 51, 52, pp. 61-63.

the breath of life, and man became a living soul." Here are the three stages of limitation: matter, organic life, the freedom of the creature. And if we want to express the coming into existence of self-determining creatures other than man, the same sort of necessity is laid upon us. We have to assume an organism and a material, as implied in the free agency of the creature.

(62.) We may now return to the question which we were about to put when this preliminary difficulty met us. The question was this: Is the conscience of humanity in harmony with the will of God? Is the power which is manifested in the universe a power favourable to righteousness? Is God good? Has natural religion an answer, and what is the answer? Of course, if God is not good the cause which I have assigned for the self-limitation of the Supreme is not the true cause. And the alternative is that He is evil, and that He has called free creatures into existence in order to the production and multiplication of wickedness; that in the unjust, not in the just, we see the manifestation of the sons of God, and that man, in so far as he is good, is engaged against God in a hopeless contest for virtue. Of course, if this were the case, then, as J. S. Mill puts it, a good man would be ready to go to hell, or whithersoever, rather than obey God.

But this alternative is too absurd to be worth considering. And yet it is really the only alternative. For at the point which we have now reached we cannot suppose God to be neither good nor evil. For that conscience of humanity which belongs, as I have said, to its continuing element, is in perpetual contest with certain impulses originally good, which humanity has cultivated downwards until they have acquired a dividing and a disorganizing power; and it is clear enough that on the issue of that contest the fate of humanity depends. And it is unreasonable to suppose that the Creator of man is indifferent to such issue, for the meaning of the contest is that humanity is making its choice between good and evil. And the making of such choice is the latest outcome of all the processes of nature that we know, and of all the creative acts which imply nature. And so to say that God is indifferent to such choice is the same as to say that there is no purpose in such processes or in such acts. And I find this incredible. And even if another man tells me that he finds it credible, he goes on for all that to assume the existence of purpose the very minute he begins to speak about nature.

All this prepares us to expect and to accept the conclusion that the Creator, in limiting Himself, is in harmony with that ideal of good which the conscience of humanity is for ever striving to realize. And when we have got so far our conclusion takes this form, that our idea of good is given us by the Creator.

(63.) It remains that we inquire what is the direct evidence (setting aside revelation) that we can bring to bear upon the question?

The most important of such evidence is to be found

in the observed relation between righteousness and the laws of nature. The "power not ourselves which makes for righteousness" is a fact which a large observation undoubtedly verifies, and the fuller the observation the more perfect is the verification.

The more extended our knowledge the firmer becomes our "assurance of the truth that the laws of nature and the inevitable working of the universe are hostile to falsehood and injustice;" that "social justice is provided for and required by the constitution of things, by the laws of an order which man did not make and cannot change."*

I do not know that this argument has ever been more forcibly put than by Bishop Butler. He supposes the case of a kingdom or society of men perfectly virtuous, and lasting throughout a succession of ages. "In such a state," he says, "there would be no such thing as faction, but men of the greatest capacity would, of course, all along have the chief direction of affairs willingly yielded to them, and they would share it among themselves without envy. . . . Public determinations would really be the result of the united wisdom of the community, and they would faithfully be executed by the united strength of it. . . . Such a kingdom would be plainly superior to all others, and the world must gradually come under its empire."† . . . The head of it would be universal

* "Atlantic Monthly," October, 1878.
† "Analogy," part i., chap. 3.

"monarch in another sense than any mortal yet has been, and the Eastern style would be literally applicable to him, that *all peoples, nations, and languages should serve him.*"

(64.) Scarcely less convincing is what has been called the "moral paradox." Although the laws of the universe appear to be so ordered that virtue must in the long run be coincident with the "greatest happiness," yet he who strives after virtue for the sake of happiness attains neither the one nor the other. Why? Because God does not immediately reward every several act of virtue with happiness. If He did, there would be no "moral paradox;" but if He did, there would soon be no virtue either. For men would in that case learn to seek virtue for the sake of happiness, and virtue so sought ceases to be virtue. But the fact is, that, although to the view which contemplates the whole universe, past, present, and future, as one, virtue must be coincident with the greatest happiness; yet in the details of time, if a man will do a good action, pain and loss are often the results upon which he may most surely reckon. Insomuch that if a man's aim be simply happiness, as men usually reckon happiness, he will find it suit such aim quite as often to be vicious as to be virtuous, and oftenest of all to strive chiefly after neither vice nor virtue, but to pass with easy and careless tolerance from either to the other. If a man will be virtuous, he must learn to disregard often all consideration of his own happiness or unhappiness. Thus the "moral paradox," which is part of the order of the universe, is a direct answer to the prayer,

> "What conscience dictates to be done,
> Or warns me not to do,
> This teach me more than hell to shun,
> That more than heaven pursue."

To the spirit of which prayer no exception at all can be taken ; and of the manner of expression of it this only needs to be said, that the one heaven which is worth "pursuing" is virtue, or godliness, or likeness to Jesus Christ, and the one hell to be shunned is the opposite of all that. These considerations point very plainly to the conclusion that God is good.

(65.) But, now, is there no appearance of evidence on the other side ? No doubt, if we think more of goodness than of happiness, we shall not hesitate to inflict pain in order to increase goodness [happiness]; but to inflict pain wantonly is assuredly not good. And the question has been asked for ages, "Does not God inflict pain wantonly?" For, they say, "If He be omnipotent, He can make men good without pain." Mr. Edwin Arnold puts the old argument as well as anyone :

> "How can it be that Brahm
> Would make a world and keep it miserable,
> Since if, all powerful, He leaves it so,
> He is not good, and if not powerful
> He is not God."*

God is surely "omnipotent ;" but omnipotence is

---

* "Light of Asia," book iii.

a word of infinite meaning, and there is no more fruitful source of confusion of thought than the attempt to deal with the infinite as if it were capable of definition. Omnipotence cannot make true two mutually exclusive statements. To say that it can is unmeaning. To say that, if God is omnipotent, He can make a triangle with only two sides, is neither true nor false; it is nonsense. But virtue implies freedom, and freedom implies the limitation of the Supreme. To say, therefore, that God can make men good without making them free, or free without limiting His own omnipotence, is to talk nonsense.

(66.) The question remains, however, "Is it worth while?" Is the whole of the disorder, sin, and pain which follow upon the self-limitation of the Supreme overbalanced by the virtue for the sake of which He has limited Himself? Is "the manifestation of the sons of God," for which creation waits, worth all the toil and travail which creation meanwhile endures? God knows, for He has done the sum. We have not the power of doing it, for the factors are not all before us; but all the evidences of God's goodness which surround us constrain us to believe that, if He had not counted the cost and found it worth while, He would not have begun the work.

(67.) But another question remains. Justice is essential to goodness. Does it accord with justice, is it fair, that anyone should be called into existence merely to "subserve another's gain?" Is God good if He allows some of His creatures to share in the pain without any prospect whatsoever of a share in the compensation? I do not think that we can estimate the meaning of this question if we include in it creatures with whom we are unable to communicate, and the nature of whose life is therefore unknown to us. But of the self-conscious creature who looks before and after, I think we may say that it is a demand of justice that he should have a share in the compensation. And such a share he cannot have if he have no life but this life. And so I think that every consideration which constrains us to believe in God's goodness, constrains us also to believe in a life after this life. And this is the strongest proof of a life after death which is known as yet to natural religion.

(68.) But still another question remains. Goodness is well worth pain. No good man can doubt that. And so one who is good will not hesitate to inflict pain for the sake of goodness. But if he does will he not feel the sufferer's pain as if it were his own pain? Will it not be his own pain? Can we attribute such sympathy to God? Surely we must if we believe Him to be good. All the evidences of God's goodness that surround us are evidences that the sufferings of the creature must reach somehow to the heart of the Creator. If God be good, surely to create was to be crucified. The triumph song of Eden implied the travail song of Gethsemane.

(69.) And this, I think, is about the last word that natural religion has to say: God is, and if God be good as He seems to be, then there must be a life after death for man, and there must be Divine sympathy with the sorrows of man.

And revealed religion, coming in at this point, and accepting the goodness of God as a fact, is bound to justify and expand these two propositions, viz.:

    I. After death man lives again; and
    II. God shares in the sorrows of mankind.

It may be said that the catholic faith is the expansion and the justification of these two propositions.

THE END.

George Robertson and Company, Printers, Melbourne.